ASTRONOMY

John Farndon
Consultant: Tim Furniss

BYEWAY
BOOKS

First published in 2003 by Miles Kelly Publishing Ltd
Bardfield Centre, Great Bardfield
Essex, CM7 4SL

This 2005 edition published by Byeway Books
Byeway Books Inc.
Lenexa, KS 66219, 866-4BYEWAY
www.byewaybooks.com

Editor: Belinda Gallagher

Design: Andy Knight

Picture Researcher: Liberty Newton

Inputting: Carol Danenbergs

Production: Estela Boulton, Eizabeth Brunwin

Library of Congress Cataloging-in-Publication Data
is on file at the Library of Congress.

ISBN 1-933581-00-X

Printed in China

2 4 6 8 10 9 7 5 3 1

The publishers would like to thank the following artists who have contributed to this book:
Kuo Kang Chen, Rob Jakeway, Janos Marffy, Rob Sheffield, Mike White

The publishers would also like to thank NASA for the generous loan of their photographs

Contents

Copernicus

● **Until the 16th century** most people thought the Earth was the center of the Universe and that everything—the Moon, Sun, planets, and stars—revolved around it.

● **Nicolaus Copernicus** was the astronomer who first suggested that the Sun was the center, and that the Earth went around the Sun. This is called the heliocentric view.

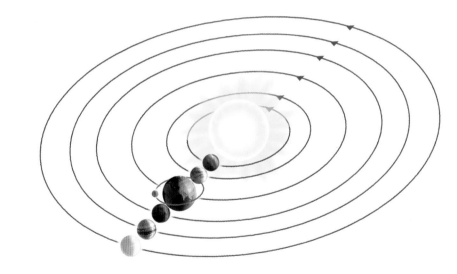

▲ *In 1543 Nicolaus Copernicus proposed a revolutionary theory, that Earth and other planets move around the Sun. Before this people had believed that the Sun and planets moved around the stationary Earth.*

▶ *"The Earth," wrote Copernicus, "carrying the Moon's path, passes in a great orbit among the other planets in an annual revolution around the Sun."*

- **Copernicus was born** on February 19, 1473 at Torun in Poland, and died on May 24, 1543.

- **Copernicus was the nephew** of a prince bishop who spent most of his life as a canon at Frauenberg Cathedral in Prussia (now Poland).

- **Copernicus described his ideas** in a book called *De revolutionibus orbium coelestium* ("On the revolutions of the heavenly spheres").

- **The Roman Catholic Church** banned Copernicus's book for almost 300 years.

- **Copernicus's ideas** came not from looking at the night sky but from studying ancient astronomy.

- **Copernicus's main clue** came from the way the planets, every now and then, seem to perform a backward loop through the sky.

- **The first proof** of Copernicus's theory came in 1609, when Galileo saw (through a telescope) moons revolving around Jupiter.

- **The change in ideas** that was brought about by Copernicus is known as the Copernican Revolution.

The night sky

- **The night sky** is brightened by the Moon and twinkling points of light.

- **Most lights** in the sky are stars. But moving, flashing lights may be satellites.

- **The brightest "stars"** in the night sky are not actually stars at all, but the planets Jupiter, Venus, Mars, and Mercury.

- **You can see** about 2,000 stars with the naked eye.

- **The pale band across** the middle of the sky is a side-on view of our own galaxy, the Milky Way.

- **The pattern of stars** in the sky is fixed, but seems to rotate (turn) through the night sky as the Earth spins.

- **It takes 23 hours 56 minutes** for the star pattern to return to the same place in the sky.

- **As Earth orbits the Sun,** our view of the stars changes and the pattern starts in a different place each night.

- **Different patterns of stars** are seen in the northern hemisphere and the southern hemisphere.

▼ *The Milky Way galaxy can be seen clearly from Earth, viewed from the side.*

◄ *Look into the night sky and you can see about 2,000 stars twinkling above you (they twinkle because of the shimmering of heat in the Earth's atmosphere). With binoculars, you can see many more. Powerful telescopes reveal not just thousands of stars but millions. Even with the naked eye, though, some of the stars you see are trillions of miles away—and their light takes millions of years to reach us.*

Astronomy

- **Astronomy is the study of the night sky**—from the planets and moons to the stars and galaxies.

- **Astronomy** is the most ancient of all the sciences, dating back tens of thousands of years.

- **The Ancient Egyptians** used their knowledge of astronomy to create their calendar and to align the pyramids.

- **The word astronomy** comes from the Ancient Greek words *astro* meaning "star" and *nomia* meaning "law."

- **Astronomers** use telescopes to study objects far fainter and smaller than can be seen with the naked eye.

- **Space objects** give out other kinds of radiation besides light, and astronomers have special equipment to detect this (see Radio and space telescopes).

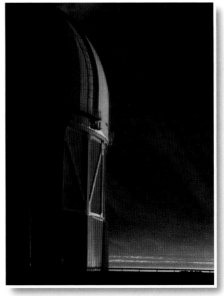

▲ *Most astronomers work in observatories far from city lights, where they can get a very clear view of the night sky.*

- **Professional astronomers** usually study photographs and computer displays instead of staring through telescopes, because most faint space objects only show up on long-exposure photographs.

- **Astronomers can spot** new objects in the night sky by laying a current photograph over an old one and looking for differences.
- **Professional astronomy** involves sophisticated equipment, but amateurs with binoculars can still occasionally make some important discoveries.

▼ *The great Egyptian pyramids at Giza are said to have been positioned to align with certain stars.*

Hipparchus

- **Hipparchus of Nicaea** was a Greek astronomer who lived in the 2nd century BC, dying in 127BC.

- **The foundations of astronomy** were laid down by Hipparchus and survived 1,500 years, until they were overthrown by the ideas of Copernicus.

- **Ancient Babylonian records** brought back by Alexander the Great from his conquests helped Hipparchus to make his observations of the stars.

- **Hipparchus was the first astronomer** to try to figure out how far away the Sun is.

- **The first star catalog,** listing 850 stars, was put together by Hipparchus.

- **Hipparchus was also the first** to identify the constellations systematically and to assess stars in terms of magnitude.

- **Hipparchus also discovered** that the relative positions of the stars on the equinoxes (March 21 and December 21) slowly shift around, taking 26,000 years to return to their original place. This is called the "precession of the equinoxes."

- **The mathematics of trigonometry** is also thought to have been invented by Hipparchus.

▲ *Some of Hipparchus'*
astronomical knowledge came from
the Sumerians, who wrote many of
their findings on clay tablets.

10

▲ *Hipparchus carried out his observations at Rhodes. He was the first to pinpoint the geographical position of places by latitude and longitude.*

Observatories

- **Observatories** are special places where astronomers study space and, to give the best view of the night sky, most are built on mountaintops far from city lights.

- **One of the largest observatory complexes** is 13,780 ft (4,200 m) above sea level, in the crater of the extinct Hawaiian volcano, Mauna Kea.

- **In most observatories,** telescopes are housed in a dome-roofed building which turns around so they can keep aiming at the same stars while the Earth rotates.

- **The oldest existing observatory** is the Tower of the Winds in Athens, Greece, which dates from 100BC.

- **In the imperial observatory** in Beijing, China, there are 500-year-old bronze astronomical instruments.

- **One of the oldest** working observatories is London's Royal Greenwich Observatory, founded in 1675.

- **The highest observatory** on the Earth is 14,108 ft (4,300 m) above sea level, near Denver, Colorado.

- **The lowest observatory** is over 1 mi (1.7 km) below sea level, in Homestake Mine, South Dakota. Its "telescope" is actually tanks of cleaning fluid which trap neutrinos from the Sun.

- **The first photographs** of the stars were taken in 1840. Nowadays, most observatories rely on photographs rather than on the eyes of astronomers.

- **Observatory photographs are made** using sensors called Charge-Coupled Devices (C.C.D.s), which give off an electrical signal when struck by light.

▲ *The Tower of the Winds observatory in Athens, Greece—the world's oldest existing observatory.*

▶ *The Kitt Peak National Observatory in Arizona.*

Telescopes

- **Optical telescopes** magnify distant objects by using lenses or mirrors to refract (bend) light rays so they focus (come together).

- **Other telescopes** detect radio waves (see Radio telescopes), X-rays (see X-rays), or other kinds of electromagnetic radiation.

- **Refracting telescopes** are optical telescopes that use lenses to refract the light rays.

- **Reflecting telescopes** are optical telescopes that refract light rays by reflecting them off curved mirrors.

▼ *This is the kind of reflecting telescope that many amateur astronomers use.*

- **Because the light rays** are folded, reflecting telescopes are shorter and fatter than refracting ones.

- **Most professional astronomers** do not gaze at the stars directly, but pick up what the telescope shows with light sensors called C.C.D.s (see Observatories).

- **Most early discoveries** in astronomy were made with refracting telescopes.

- **Modern observatories** use gigantic reflector dishes made up of hexagons of glass or coated metal.

- **Large telescope dishes** are continually monitored and tweaked by computers to make sure that the reflector's mirrored surface stays completely smooth.

▼ *The giant mosaic mirror of a huge telescope at the Smithsonian Observatory, Arizona.*

····FASCINATING FACT····
Telescope dishes have to be made accurate
to within less than a billionth of an inch.

Herschel

- **William Herschel** (1738–1822) was an amateur astronomer who built his own, very powerful telescope in his home in Bath, England.

- **Until Herschel's time,** astronomers assumed there were just seven independent objects in the sky: the Moon, the Sun, and five planets.

- **The five known planets** were Mercury, Venus, Mars, Jupiter and Saturn.

- **Uranus,** the sixth planet, was discovered by William Herschel in 1781.

- **At first, Herschel** had thought that the dot of light he could see through his telescope was a star. But when he looked more closely, he saw a tiny disk instead of a point of light. When he looked the next night, the "star" had moved—this meant that it had to be a planet.

- **Herschel wanted to name** the planet George, after King George III, but Uranus was eventually chosen.

- **Herschel's partner** in his discoveries was his sister Caroline (1750–1848), another great astronomer, who cataloged (listed) all the stars of the northern hemisphere.

- **Herschel's son John** cataloged the stars of the southern hemisphere.

- **Herschel himself added** to the catalog of nebulae.

- **Herschel was also the first** to explain that the Milky Way is our view of a galaxy shaped "like a grindstone."

▲ *William Herschel was one of the greatest astronomers. With the help of his sister Caroline, he discovered Uranus in 1781. He later identified two of the moons of Uranus and Saturn.*

▶ *The huge, extremely powerful telescope that Herschel built at his own home, in Bath, England.*

Space telescopes

- **Space telescopes** are launched as satellites so we can study the Universe without interference from Earth's atmosphere.

- **The first space telescope** was Copernicus, sent up in 1972.

- **The most famous** is the Hubble space telescope, launched from a space shuttle in 1990.

- **Different space telescopes** study all the different forms of radiation that make up the electromagnetic spectrum.

- **The COBE satellite** picks up microwave radiation which may be left over from the Big Bang.

- **The IRAS satellite** studied infrared radiation from objects as small as space dust.

- **Space telescopes** that study ultraviolet rays from the stars included the International Ultraviolet Explorer (I.U.E.), launched in 1978.

- **Helios** was one of many space telescopes studying the Sun.

- **X-rays** can only be picked up by space telescopes such as the Einstein, ROSAT, and XTE satellites.

- **Gamma rays** can only be picked up by space telescopes like the Compton Gamma-Ray Observatory.

▶ *The Hubble space telescope's main mirror was faulty when it was launched, but a replacement was fitted by shuttle astronauts in 1994.*

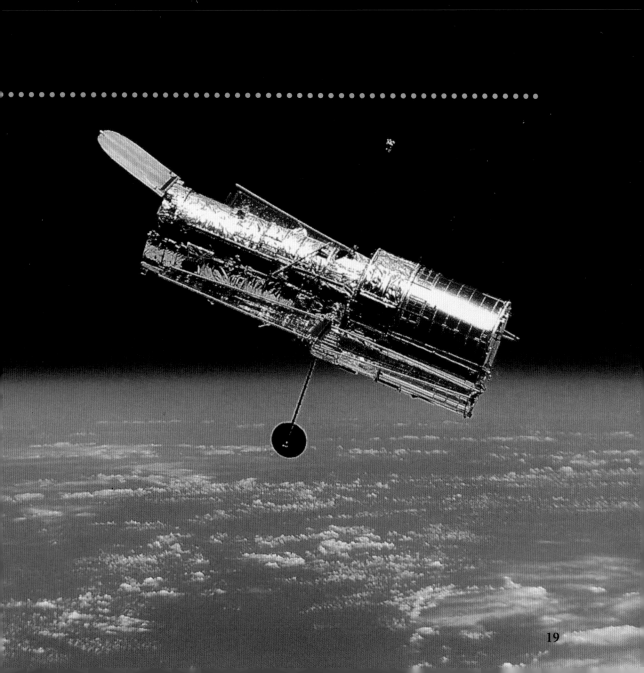

19

Galileo

- **Galileo Galilei** (1564–1642) was a great Italian mathematician and astronomer.

- **Galileo was born** in Pisa on February 15, 1564, in the same year as William Shakespeare.

- **The pendulum clock** was invented by Galileo after watching a swinging lamp in Pisa Cathedral in 1583.

- **Galileo's experiments** with balls rolling down slopes laid the basis for our understanding of how gravity affects acceleration (speeding up).

- **Learning of the telescope's invention,** Galileo made his own to look at the Moon, Venus, and Jupiter.

- **Galileo described his observations** of space in a book called *The Starry Messenger*, published in 1613.

- **Through his telescope** Galileo saw that Jupiter has four moons (see Jupiter's Galilean moons). He also saw that Venus has phases (as our Moon does).

- **Jupiter's moon and Venus's phases** were the first visible evidence of Copernicus' theory that the Earth moves round the Sun. Galileo also believed this.

- **Galileo was declared a heretic** in 1616 by the Catholic Church, for his support of Copernican theory. Later, threatened with torture, Galileo was forced to deny that the Earth orbits the Sun. Legend has it he muttered "eppur si muove" ("yet it does move") afterward.

▲ *One of the most brilliant scientists of all time, Galileo ended his life imprisoned (in his villa near Florence) for his beliefs.*

▲ *Galileo studied the skies through his telescope, which he demonstrated to members of the Venetian senate.*

. . . **FASCINATING FACT** . . .
Only on October 13, 1992 was the sentence of the Catholic Church on Galileo retracted.

21

Hubble

- **Edwin Hubble** (1889–1953) was an American who trained in law at Chicago and Oxford, and was also a great boxer before he turned to astronomy.

- **Until the early 20th century**, astronomers thought that our galaxy was all there was to the Universe.

- **In the 1920s Hubble** showed that the fuzzy patches of light once thought to be nebulae were in fact other galaxies far beyond the Milky Way.

- **In 1929 Hubble** measured the red shift of 18 galaxies, and showed that they were all moving away from us.

- **Red shift showed Hubble** that the farther away a galaxy is, the faster it is moving.

- **The ratio of a galaxy's distance** to the speed it is moving away from us is now known as Hubble's Law.

▲ *One of Hubble's earliest achievements was to show that some "nebulae" were really other galaxies.*

- **Hubble's Law** showed that the Universe is getting bigger, and so must have started very small. This led to the idea of the Big Bang.

- **The figure given** by Hubble's law is Hubble's constant and is about 25–50 mi/sec (40–80 km/sec) per megaparsec.

- **In the 1930s Hubble** showed that the Universe is isotropic (the same in all directions).

- **Hubble space telescope** is named after Edwin Hubble.

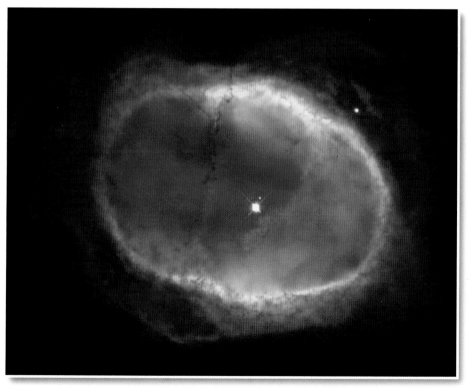

▲ *Pictures of planetary nebulae, as observed by the Hubble space telescope.*

Radio telescopes

- **Radio telescopes** are telescopes that pick up radio waves instead of light waves.

- **Radio telescopes,** like reflecting telescopes (see Telescopes), have a big dish to collect and focus data.

- **At the center of its dish,** a radio telescope has an antenna which picks up radio signals.

- **Because radio waves** are much longer than light waves, radio telescope dishes are very big—often as much as 330 ft (100 m) across.

- **Instead of one big dish,** some radio telescopes use an array (collection) of small, linked dishes. The farther apart the dishes are, the sharper the image.

- **The Very Long Baseline Array** (V.L.B.A.) is made of ten dishes scattered all the way across the United States.

- **Radio astronomy** led to the discovery of pulsars and background radiation from the Big Bang.

- **Radio galaxies** are very distant and only faintly visible (if at all), but they can be detected because they give out radio waves.

- **Radio astronomy** proved that the Milky Way is a disk-shaped galaxy with spiraling arms.

...FASCINATING FACT...

At 1,000 ft (305 m) across, the Arecibo radio telescope in Puerto Rico is the largest dish telescope in the world.

▼ *Many radio telescopes use an array of dishes linked by a process called interferometry.*

Kepler

- **Johannes Kepler** (1571–1630) was the German astronomer who discovered the basic rules about the way the planets move.

- **Kepler got his ideas** from studying Mars' movement.

- **Before Kepler's discoveries,** people thought that the planets moved in circles.

- **Kepler discovered** that the true shape of the planets' orbits is elliptical (oval). This is Kepler's first law.

- **Kepler's second law** is that the speed of a planet through space varies with its distance from the Sun.

- **A planet moves fastest** when its orbit brings it nearest to the Sun (called its perihelion). It moves slowest when it is furthest from the Sun (called its aphelion).

- **Kepler's third law** is that a planet's period—the time it takes to complete its yearly orbit of the Sun —depends on its distance from the Sun.

- **Kepler's third law states** that the square of a planet's period is proportional to the cube of its average distance from the Sun.

- **Kepler believed** that the planets made harmonious music as they moved, "the music of the spheres."

- **Kepler also wrote a book** about measuring how much wine there was in wine casks, which proved to be important for the mathematics of calculus.

▲ *Despite almost losing his eyesight and the use of his hands through smallpox at the age of three, Johannes Kepler became an assistant to the great Danish astronomer Tycho Brahe, and took over his work when Brahe died.*

▲ *Johannes Kepler was sponsored in his research by Emperor Rudolph II. Here they discuss Kepler's discoveries of planetary motion.*

Zodiac

- **The zodiac** is the band of constellations the Sun appears to pass in front of during the year, as the Earth orbits the Sun. It lies along the ecliptic.

- **The ecliptic** is the plane (level) of the Earth's orbit around the Sun. The Moon and all planets but Pluto lie in the same plane.

- **The Ancient Greeks** divided the zodiac into 12 parts, named after the constellation they saw in each part. These are the signs of the zodiac.

- **The 12 constellations of the zodiac** are Aries, Taurus, Gemini, Cancer, Leo, Virgo, Libra, Scorpio, Sagittarius, Capricorn, Aquarius, and Pisces.

- **Astrologers** are people who believe that the movements of planets and stars have an effect on people's lives. They are not scientists.

- **For astrologers**, all the constellations of the zodiac are equal in size. The ones used by astronomers are not.

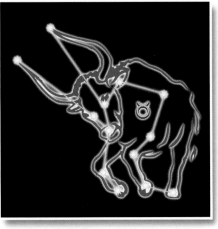

▲ *Taurus, the bull*

- **The Earth has tilted** slightly since ancient times and the constellations no longer correspond to the zodiac.

- **A 13th constellation, Ophiuchus,** now lies within the zodiac, but astrologers ignore it.

- **The dates that the Sun** seems to pass in front of each constellation no longer match the dates astrologers use.

◀ Leo, the lion

▼ Libra, the scales

◀ Aries, the ram

▲ *The zodiac signs are imaginary symbols that ancient astronomers linked to star patterns.*

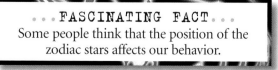

. . . **FASCINATING FACT** . . .
Some people think that the position of the
zodiac stars affects our behavior.

Red shift

- **When distant galaxies** are moving away from us, the very, very, fast light waves they give off are stretched out behind them, since each bit of the light wave is being sent from a little bit farther away.

- **When the light waves** from distant galaxies are stretched out in this way, they look redder. This is called red shift.

- **Red shift** was first described by Czech mathematician Christian Doppler in 1842.

- **Edwin Hubble** showed that a galaxy's red shift is proportional to its distance. So the further away a galaxy is, the greater its red shift—and the faster it must be zooming away from us. This is Hubble's Law.

- **The increase of red shift** with distance proved that the Universe is growing bigger.

- **Only nearby galaxies** show no red shift at all.

- **The record red shift** is 4.25, from the quasar 8C 1435 + 63. It is 96 percent of the speed of light.

- **Red shift** can be caused by the expansion of the Universe, gravity or the effect of relativity (see Einstein).

- **Black holes** may create large red shifts.

▶ *Red Shift occurs as distant galaxies move away from us. The farther away a galaxy is, the greater its red shift.*

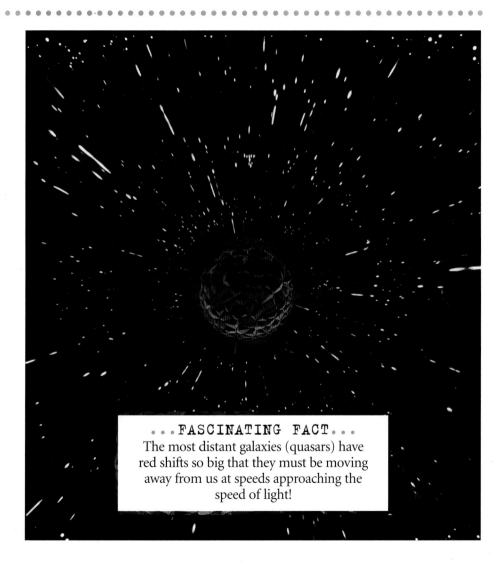

...FASCINATING FACT...
The most distant galaxies (quasars) have red shifts so big that they must be moving away from us at speeds approaching the speed of light!

Light-years

- **Distances in space** are so vast that the fastest thing in the Universe—light—is used to measure them.

- **The speed of light** is about 186,410 mi/sec (300,000 km/sec).

- **A light-second** is the distance light travels in a second.

- **A light-year** is the distance light travels in a year—5.9 trillion mi (9.46 trillion km). Light-years are one of the standard distance measurements in astronomy.

- **It takes about eight minutes** for light from the Sun to reach us on Earth.

- **Light takes 5.46 years** to reach us from the Sun's nearest star, Proxima Centauri. This means the star is 5.46 light-years away—more than 32 trillion mi (51 trillion km).

- **We see Proxima Centauri** as it was 5.46 years ago, because its light takes 5.46 years to reach us.

- **The star Deneb** is 1,800 light-years away, which means we see it as it was when Septimus Severius was ruling in Rome (AD200.)

▲ *Distances in space are so vast that they are measured in light-years, the distance light travels in a year.*

- **With powerful telescopes,** astronomers can see galaxies 2 billion light-years away. This means we see them as they were when the only life forms on Earth were bacteria.

- **Parsecs** may also be used to measure distances. They originally came from parallax shift measurements. A light-year is 0.3066 parsecs.

Brightest Stars

Name	Star of Constellation	Apparent Magnitude	Distance Light Years
Sirius	alpha Canis Major	-1.46	8.6
Canopus	alpha Carinae	-0.72	110
	alpha Centauri	-0.01	4.37
Arcturus	alpha Bootis	-0.04	36
Vega	alpha Lyrae	-0.03	26
Capella	alpha Aurigae	-0.08	45
Rigel	beta Orionis	-0.12	850
Procyon	alpha Canis Minoris	-0.8	11.4
Achernar	alpha Eridani	-0.46	118
Hadar	beta Centauri	-0.66	520
Betelgeuse	alpha Orionis	-0.70	650
Altair	alpha Aquilae	-0.77	16
Aldebaran	alpha Tauri	-0.85	64
Acrux	alpha Crucis	-0.87	370
Antares	alpha Scorpii	-0.92	430
Spica	alpha Virginis	1.00	260
Pollux	beta Geminorum	1.14	35
Fomalhaut	alpha Piscis Austrani	1.16	23
Deneb	alpha Cygni	1.25	1,500
	beta Crucis	1.28	490
Regulus	alpha Leonis	1.35	84
Adhara	epsilon Canis Majoris	1.50	680
Castor	alpha Geminorum	1.59	45
Shaula	lambda Scorpii	1.62	610
Bellatrix	lambda Orionis	1.64	470

Note: not all of these stars can be seen in the northern hemisphere

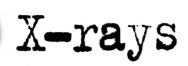

X-rays

- **X-rays** are electromagnetic rays whose waves are shorter than ultraviolet rays and longer than gamma rays.

- **X-rays in space** may be produced by very hot gases well over 1.8 million°F (1 million°C).

- **X-rays are also made** when electrons interact with a magnetic field in synchrotron radiation.

- **X-rays cannot get through** Earth's atmosphere, so astronomers can only detect them using space telescopes such as ROSAT.

- **X-ray sources** are stars and galaxies that give out X-rays.

- **The first and brightest X-ray source** found (apart from the Sun) was the star Scorpius X-1, in 1962. Now tens of thousands are known, although most are weak.

- **The remnants of supernovae** such as the Crab nebula are strong sources of X-rays.

- **The strongest sources of X-rays** in our galaxy are X-ray binaries like Scorpius X-1 and Cygnus X-1. Some are thought to contain black holes.

- **X-ray binaries** pump out 1,000 times as much X-ray radiation as the Sun does.

- **X-ray galaxies** harboring big black holes are powerful X-ray sources outside our galaxy.

▶ *The Sun was the first X-ray source to be discovered.*

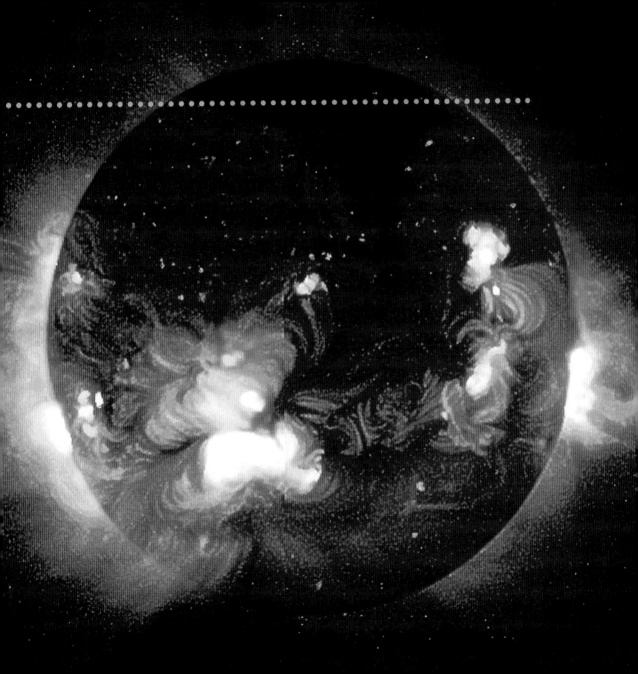

Newton

- **Isaac Newton** (1642–1722) was the British scientist who first explained how gravity works.

- **Newton's ideas** were inspired by seeing an apple fall from a tree in the garden of his home in Lincolnshire.

- **Newton also discovered** that sunlight can be split into a spectrum made of all the colors of the rainbow.

- **Newton showed** why gravity makes things fall to the ground and planets orbit the Sun.

- **Newton realized** that a planet's orbit depends on its mass and its distance from the Sun.

- **The further apart** and the lighter two objects are, the weaker is the pull of gravity between them.

- **Newton worked out** that you can calculate the pull of gravity between two objects by multiplying their respective mass then divide by the square of the distance between them.

- **This calculation** allows astronomers to predict precisely the movement of every planet, star, and galaxy in the Universe.

▲ *If ordinary white light is passed through a glass prism, it splits up into all the different colors of the light spectrum.*

- **Using Newton's formula for gravity,** astronomers have detected previously unknown stars and planets, including Neptune and Pluto, from the effect of their gravity on other space objects.

- **Newton's three laws of motion** showed that every single movement in the Universe can be calculated mechanically.

▲ *Newton's theory of gravity showed for the first time why the Moon stays in its orbit around the Earth, and how the gravitational pull between the Earth and the Moon could be worked out mathematically.*

▲ *Newton was made Lucasian professor of mathematics at Cambridge University in 1669, where he studied how and why things in our Universe move.*

Voyagers 1 and 2

- The *Voyagers* are a pair of unmanned U.S. space probes, launched to explore the outer planets.

- *Voyager 1* was launched on September 5, 1977. It flew past Jupiter in March 1979 and Saturn in November 1980, then headed onward on a curved path that will take it out of the Solar System altogether.

- *Voyager 2* travels more slowly. Although launched two weeks earlier than *Voyager 1*, it did not reach Jupiter until July 1979 and Saturn until August 1981.

- The *Voyagers* used the "slingshot" of Jupiter's gravity to hurl them on toward Saturn.

- **While *Voyager 1* headed out** of the Solar System, *Voyager 2* flew past Uranus in January 1986 and Neptune on August 24, 1989. It took the first close-up photographs of the two planets.

◀ *Io, Jupiter's orange moon.* Voyager 2 *discovered sulfur volcanoes on this moon, in 1979.*

- The *Voyagers* revealed volcanoes on Io, one of Jupiter's Galilean moons.

- *Voyager 2* found ten unknown moons around Uranus.

- *Voyager 2* found six unknown moons and three rings around Neptune.

▶ Voyager 2 *reached Neptune in 1989, revealing a wealth of new information about this distant planet.*

...FASCINATING FACT...

Voyager 2 will beam back data until 2020 as it travels beyond the edges of the Solar System.

Index